Blossoming Love

Flowers expressing vows

Edwin R. Molenaar

Photography

Tomoyuki Sasaki

Marc Dorleijn

Randy R.A. Gibbs

Edwin R. Molenaar

stichting kunstboek

Flowers expressing vows

Undertakings

My love of nature began as an undertaking of my grandfather. When I was young, he taught me how amazing the out-of-doors could be. As a child, I grew up with all kinds of animals and was surrounded by nature, both inside the house and outside. Nature was my favorite place to be: while other children were playing, I spent my time in the forest near the seashore with my nose in a book, learning more about life and the forces of nature.

At junior high school, the headmaster noticed my interest in nature and suggested to my parents that I would be better off going to a trade school rather than to an academically oriented high school. So, I entered an agricultural college to study gardening, forestry and floral design.

When my teacher asked for my opinion on flowers and flower decoration, I told him with the utmost confidence and authority that flowers were boring. I had no interest in flowers at all.

At the age of twelve, a dream to work with nature began to take shape: I decided that I would become a forester and save the Amazon. However, my teacher of floristry, sensing a hidden talent, took it upon himself to open my eyes to the possibility of another career. When he asked for my opinion on flowers and flower decoration, I told him with the utmost confidence and authority that flowers were boring. I had no interest in flowers at all. But, little by little, he managed to change my opinion and fill in the gaps in my knowledge. He had been the owner of a flower shop and still made some decorations once in a while. By assisting my teacher with seasonal projects, I developed a passion for floral design and experienced the joy of customer satisfaction. After three years, my views on flowers and floristry had changed completely. Instead of becoming a forester, I set out on an undertaking of my own: to become a floral designer.

Declarations

I wish to thank the brides and grooms as well as their families for allowing me and a photographer into their private ceremonies and for consenting to share these design ideas with others. I am deeply grateful for their understanding and enthusiasm in this project.

It is my profound belief that the flower design as chosen by the bride and groom is expressed through the eyes and hands of the designer. It communicates to both family and friends the couple's vision of their new life together.

Rather than focusing on the risks, I like to look at the results and the chance to elevate the event far above the couple's expectations.

Here in Japan, I encounter numerous florists with about three standard designs they repeat over and over again throughout the year. These 'fast-flower' designers may claim that, after all, the design is new to each new customer and that a limited choice prevents the florist from misinterpreting the wishes of the customer — wishes that are effectively ignored. Although it might be true that few couples would notice the repetition, I think that it is impossible to capture with a handful of designs the distinctive spark and nuance that each couple presents to the world — no matter how inspired the original concept might be. In fact, custom-design makes our business fun.

Rather than focusing on the risks, I like to look at the results and the chance to elevate the event far above the couple's expectations. In this way, I can contribute to the uniqueness of their wedding.

Vows

In my opinion, one of the prerequisites of good floral design is the absence of any expression of the designer's personal feelings. The basics of any floral design, of course, are the materials, consisting of head flowers, sub flowers and side materials (greenery). The head flower, the star of the design, can be compared with a solo performer; the sub flowers are the choir and the side materials are the backing vocals. The head flower need not even be a flower; it could be an idea suggested by the bride or groom, or a wedding dress, or any other personal element linked to the participants.

In custom-design, the first unspoken question should be 'what is the head flower?'. In the first example in this book, *Mille Fleurs* (one thousand flowers) — one of my favorite approaches — there is no head flower in the literal sense of the word. In this design approach, the bride, the room or the event itself can become the head flower — whatever has the most sense for the customer.

When interviewing new customers, it is important to find out what the figurative 'head flower' will be. This way, the customers themselves contribute to a more personal design, adding depth and meaningfulness to the ceremony. Only then can a floral designer be satisfied with the design he or she has created.

Edwin R. Molenaar

Mille fleurs

I have been working together with Kikuchi-san, beverage manager at the Hotel Bleston Court in Japan, for over five years. He is a very refined man, with an eye for details and an almost obsessive sense of style. When he told me he was getting married, I expected to receive a highly detailed outline of the wedding. Instead, our meeting was one of the shortest in my career. 'Mr. Molenaar', he said, 'since you know me so well, your design will capture my wishes'. However, because he gave me complete freedom, the design turned out to be one of the most difficult creations in my career.

His fiancée, Yuri, is a very cheerful and charming lady. She put a lot of special care into her wedding and went to more than twenty shops to find her wedding dress. I realized that her dress must become the head flower of the concept and that all other flowers would be an extension of that dress.

For this wedding, I chose a mille fleurs design. As a finishing touch, decorative candles were put on the main table — as they were always a favorite of Kikuchi's. Kikuchi and I had worked together on a thousand designs, lending a special significance to the 'thousand flowers' theme. We had always enjoyed the effect of the colors in each creation, and I fondly recalled how much fun it had been.

Acacia dealbata
Bouvardia
Bulbinella
Chrysanthemum
Delphinium
Leucothoe walteri 'Rainbow'
Lupinus hartwegii
Nigella
Ranunculus asiaticus
Rosa 'Ranuncula'
Scilla peruviana
Senecio cruentus
Tanacetum parthenium
Zantedeschia
▽

Davallia mariesii ▷
Ixia
Kalanchoe blossfeldiana
Lathyrus latifolius
Lathyrus odoratus
Ranunculus asiaticus
Rosa 'Purple Heart'
Scilla peruviana
Tulipa
Zantedeschia

Acacia dealbata
Bouvardia
Bulbinella
Chrysanthemum
Delphinium
Leucothoe walteri 'Rainbow'
Lupinus hartwegii
Nigella
Ranunculus asiaticus
Rosa 'Ranuncula'
Scilla peruviana
Senecio cruentus
Tanacetum parthenium
Zantedeschia

Bouvardia
Bulbinella
Chrysanthemum
Helichrysum petiolare
Ixia
Leucothoe walteri 'Rainbow'
Lupinus hartwegii
Nigella
Scilla peruviana
Senecio cruentus

Bouvardia
Davallia mariesii
Ixia
Kalanchoe blossfeldiana
Lathyrus latifolius
Lathyrus odoratus
Rosa 'Purple Heart'
Tulipa
Zantedeschia

Bouvardia
Bulbinella
Chrysanthemum
Helichrysum petiolare
Ixia
Leucothoe walteri 'Rainbow'
Lupinus hartwegii
Nigella
Scilla peruviana
Senecio cruentus

Antirrhinum majus
Eucalyptus gunnii
Eucalyptus niphophila
Kochia sedifolia
Tillandsia usneoides ▷
▽

△
‹ Actinotus helianthi
Amaranthus caudatus
Clematis integrifolia
Clematis jackmanii
Milla biflora
Rosa 'Spray White'
Rosmarinus officinalis
Salvia leucantha
Scabiosa caucasica
Veronica

Astilbe 'Peach Blossom' | Cotinus coggygria |
Daphne burkwoodii | Nerine bowdenii |
Rosa 'Mimi Eden' | Vinca

Aeschynanthus | Amaranthus caudatus |
Ceratopetalum gummiferum | Dahlia | Hedera helix |
Rosa 'Ambridge Rose' | Senecio herreianus |
Veronica | Vinca

Cyperus papyrus | Daucus carota | Lysimachia clethroides | Papaver somniferum | Polygonum cuspidatum | Rosa 'Avalanche' | Viburnum tinus | Xanthorroea 'Australis'

Fairy's picnic

The bride has been employed with my company for a number of years. She met her future husband at the opening party of one of our new shops in the mountain resort town of Karuizawa, outside of Tokyo.

The bride asked me for a design in which she would be the fairy princess. Also, she wanted the reception to be like a picnic. By that, I knew she did not want a formal party, but one full of whimsy and surprise, which I tried to deliver in the table details.

The wedding ceremony took place in the Karuizawa Stone Church, one of the finest creations of the organic school architect Kendrick Bangs Kellogg. It was the first time I made a design for this chapel, which is, by any standard, an architectural marvel. Water, stone and greenery, the three architectural elements of this chapel, were the basis of my inspiration for this wedding.

Both my acquaintance with the bride and the excitement of working in such a wondrous environment encouraged me to design a fantasy-filled concept — assuring of course that all elements remained subservient to the fairy princess in their midst.

Alchemilla mollis
Astilbe arendsii
Astrantia major
Convallaria majalis
Cotinus coggygria
Eustoma grandiflorum
Kerria japonica 'Variegata'
Lysimachia clethroides
Nigella damascene
Rosa 'Bianca'
< Xanthorroea 'Australis'

Alchemilla mollis >
Amaranthus caudatus
Eustoma
Gardenia jasminoides
Hosta sieboldiana
Hydrangea quercifolia
Ornithogalum
Polygonum cuspidatum (dry)
Rubus palmatus
Stemona japonica
Typha latifolia

Astrantia major >
Nigella
Rosa 'Extreme'
Stachys byzantina

Astrantia major
Clematis glaucophylla
Eustoma
Hyacinthoides hispanica
Nigella
Rosa 'Extreme'
Rumohra adiantiformis
Spiraea japonica
Stachys byzantina
▽

△
Amaranthus caudatus
Hosta sieboldiana
Paeonia suffruticosa
Tamarix chinensis

Aquilegia vulgaris
Clematis glaucophylla
Enkianthus perulatus
Gramineae (Grass)
Hydrangea
Myrtus communis
Rosa 'Rose Yumi'
Scirpus tabernaemontani

Aquilegia vulgaris
Clematis glaucophylla
Enkianthus perulatus
Gramineae (Grass)
Hydrangea
Myrtus communis
Rosa 'Rose Yumi'
Scirpus tabernaemontani

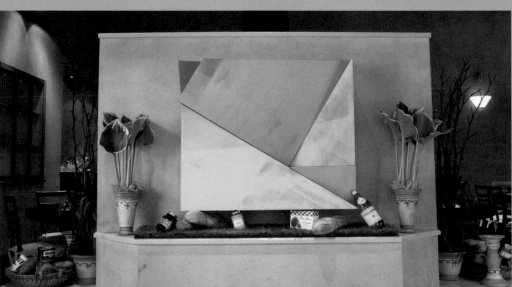

∧
< Astilbe
Hosta 'Albo-Marginata'
Polygonum
Rubus thibetanus
Scabiosa atropurpurea
Setaria italica
Xerophyllum tenax

Dracaena marginata 'Bicolor'
Hedera helix 'Goldchild'
Polygonatum odoratum
Rumohra adiantiformis
Rosa 'Emerald'
Rosa 'Eskimo'
Rosa 'Tineke'
Senecio cineraria
◁ Setaria italica
▽

Dracaena marginata 'Bicolor'
Hedera helix 'Goldchild'
Polygonatum odoratum
Rumohra adiantiformis
Rosa 'Emerald'
Rosa 'Eskimo'
Rosa 'Tineke'
Senecio cineraria
Setaria italica ▷
◁ ▽

Bessera elegans | Celosia argentea | Cornus alba |
Eucalyptus populus | Mentha | Phalaenopsis
'Brother Pepride' | Sedum sieboldii | Senecio cineraria

Amaranthus caudatus | Astilbe | Bouvardia |
Cosmos atrosanguineus | Cotinus coggygria |
Hyacinthus orientalis | Jasminum polyanthum |
Polyscias balfouriana | Ranunculus | Rosa 'Tamango' |
Rosa 'Vintage Red' | Scabiosa atropurpurea

Alium hybrids | Calocephalus brownii | Echinacea purpurea | Hippeastrum | Hydrangea | Medinilla magnifica | Monarda didyma |
Paeonia lactiflora | Phlox stolonifera | Rubus fruticosus | Salix chaenomeloides | Setaria italica | Thymus serphyllum

Purple, white and green

She chose purple and white, the colors of royalty. It was the first time in my career that a couple expressed its desires in terms of colors, which was quite a challenge to me. In Buddhist ceremonies, purple and white are the colors of mourning and death — hardly the emotions you want to evoke on the joyful occasion of a wedding — so we agreed upon using green as a balancing color. Also, I learned that the bride was from Nagoya, meaning that richly embellished elegance would barely be enough. I suspected this from experience, and it was confirmed by conversation and observation.

Then I set out, with delicate sleight-of-hand, to give her the elegance she sought, while distracting the guests from mournful thoughts of funeral and death.

It was interesting to learn that the groom was an enthusiastic adventurer and backpack-traveler, happiest when stuffing some T-shirts into a backpack and traveling about, so I incorporated his free spirit into the selection of sub flowers and side materials. The bride's beaming smile told me it worked, and none of the grandmothers fainted upon seeing the colors ...

Welcome to Our Wedding Party
Takehiko & Sayaka
12th November 2006

Brassica oleracea
Cordyline fruticosa 'Red Edge'
Gynura aurantiaca 'Purple Passion'
Lathyrus latifolius
Lathyrus odoratus
Rosa 'Avalanche'
Stemona japonica
Syringa vulgaris
Talinum crassifolium
Viburnum opulus

Brassica oleracea
Eustoma grandiflorum
Gynura aurantiaca 'Purple Passion'
Hedera helix
Lysimachia clethroides
Muehlenbeckia complexa
Paeonia lactiflora
Pittosporum tenuifolium
Rosa 'Yves Piaget'
Syringa vulgaris
Viola tricolor 'Hortensis'

Adenanthos cygnorum
Cordyline fruticosa 'Red Edge'
Galax urceolata
Pittosporum tenuifolium
Rosa 'Avalanche'
Stachys byzantina

Ceratopetalum gummiferum
Galax urceolata
Pittosporum tenuifolium
Senecio cineraria ▷

Bouvardia
Brassica oleracea
Ceratopetalum gummiferum
Cordyline fruticosa
'Red Edge'
Dendrobium unicum
Eustoma grandiflorum
Globba magnifica
Gynura aurantiaca
'Purple Passion'
Hedera helix
Lathyrus latifolius

Lathyrus odoratus
Lysimachia clethroides
Muehlenbeckia complexa
Paeonia lactiflora
Piper nigrum
Pittosporum tenuifolium
Pteris cretica
Rosa 'Avalanche'
Rosa 'Grandma'
Stemona japonica
Syringa vulgaris
Viburnum opulus

Ceratopetalum gummiferum
Galax urceolata
Pittosporum tenuifolium
Senecio cineraria
▽

◁ Actinotus helianthi
Dendrobium unicum
Hydrangea macrophylla
Viola tricolor 'Hortensis'

59

Asplenium nidus
Cordyline fruticosa 'Red Edge'
Gynura aurantiaca 'Purple Passion'
Jasminum humile 'Glabrum'
Lysimachia clethroides
Piper nigrum
Rosa 'Avalanche'
Rumohra adiantiformis
∨

◁ Rosmarinus officinalis
Rosa 'Avalanche'
Rumohra adiantiformis

Ceratopetalum gummiferum
Dendrobium unicum
Globba magnifica
Pisum sativu
▽

Eustoma grandiflorum
Muehlenbeckia complexa
Panicum capillare

Aerva javanica 'Silver Cat'
Hydrangea macrophylla
Lathyrus latifolius
Lathyrus odoratus
Muehlenbeckia complexa
Tillandsia usneoides
Viola tricolor 'Hortensis'

Ceratopetalum gummiferum >
Hypericum inodorum
Pittosporum tenuifolium

Ceratopetalum gummiferum >
Dendrobium unicum
Globba magnifica
Hyacinthus orientalis
Jasminum humile 'Glabrum'
Livistona chinensis
Livistona rotundifolia
Paeonia lactiflora
Rosmarinus officinalis

Asparagus densiflorus
Bouvardia
Brassica oleracea
Celosia argentea
Cyrtomium falcatum
Dahlia hortensis
Enkianthus perulatus
Eustoma grandiflorum
Kalanchoe blossfeldiana
Lathyrus odoratus
∨

Hyacinthus orientalis
Hydrangea macrophylla
Nephrolepis exaltata 'Sonata'
Pittosporum tenuifolium
Ranunculus asiaticus
Rosa 'Cadillac'
Senecio cineraria
Skimmia japonica 'Rubella'
Trifolium incarnatum
Vaccaria pyramidata ▷
∨

Ranunculus asiaticus

Cissus rhombifolia | Panicum capillare |
Rosa 'Emerald' | Stemona japonica | Sirene vulgaris

Aechmea 'Blue Rain' | Agapanthus | Asclepias | Carthamus tinctorius | Hedera helix 'Arborescens' | Kniphofia | Phlox paniculata | Veronica

English rose garden

The bride has known our shop in Yokohama for a long time and had been dreaming of ordering her ideal wedding bouquet with us. However, in Japan, the hotel rigidly controls all aspects of the wedding ceremony, especially the suppliers. She knew that she could not appoint her favorite flower designer, but she was not aware of the fact that I had a flower shop in the hotel. It was a complete surprise for her to discover that I would not only create her dream bouquet, but also that I would organize the whole wedding decoration!

Upon customer request, I used the rose *Romantic Curiosa*, and, instead of creating an ornate design, I incorporated it into a rose garden look. The wedding bouquet required some special thought, but was a pleasure to create.

The main challenge was the use of the rose itself, which varies widely in color, depending on the climate and the location. What if it did not match the bride's ideal? And what about the guests … half of them would be wearing black kimonos, known for modernist austerity — how could I take them all to Southern England on a summer's day? But somehow, we all arrived …

Gardenia jasminoides
Hedera helix 'Lemon Swirl'
Hosta 'American Halo'
Rosa multiflora
Rosa 'Ballerina' ▷

Amaranthus caudatus
Hydrangea macrophylla
Myrtus communis
Polygonum cuspidatum (dry)
Polygonatum odoratum
Rosa 'Ballerina'
Rosa 'Littlewoods'
Rosa 'Petit Folie'
Rosa 'Romantic Curiosa'
Rosa 'Rumarosa'
Rubus trifidus

Gardenia jasminoides >
Rubus trifidus

Rosa 'Ballerina'
Rubus trifidus

Bouvardia
Celosia argentea
Cordyline compacta
Dianthus
Dhalia 'Magic Moment'
Enkianthus perulatus
Erica gracilis
Eustoma grandiflorum
Ficus pumila
Helleborus orientalis
Hydrangea macrophylla
▽

Kochia sedifolia
Microsorum musifolium
Philodendron andreanum
Piper nigrum
Polygonum capitatum
Rosa 'Titanic'
Sarracenia leucophylla
Serruria florida
Skimmia japonica
Tillandsia xerographica
Zantedeschia araceae ▷
▽

Astrantia carniolica 'Rubra' | Centaurea suaveolens |
Cissus antarctica | Corynanthera flava |
Cosmos atrosanguineus | Jasminum polyanthum |
Parthenocissus 'Sugarvine' | Ranunculus 'Frejus' |
Rosachinensis minima 'Teddy Bear' |
Rosmarinus officinalis | Stemoca japonica

Cissus antarctica | Eucalyptus polyanthemos |
Fragaria xananassa | Hydrangea macrophylla |
Muscari ameniacum | Rosa 'Andalucia' | Veronica |
Vitis vinifera

Amarcrinum howardii | Cardiospermum halicacabum |
Coronilla valentina | Helleborus orientalis |
Ophiopogon malayanus | Salix matsudana 'Tortuosa' |
Scabiosa atropurpurea

Flowers expressing vows

Before you read any further, stop and see if you can find the difference between this photo section and the ones before.

Did you find it? Every design in this book was created for a couple in love, except for this one, which was meant as an experimental exercise. In this design, I challenged myself to play with an assortment of elements and I explored how the overall effect of the design was changed by simply substituting a strong color, or by using unusual materials or an uncommon style.

By no means does this experimental work represent my 'ideal wedding', nor does it show off my best work — as it was composed beyond the confines of client demands. From my point of view, the customer is the beginning and end of any design, and it would be arrogant to consider as my best designs those that were not meant for a customer.

I hope that this glimpse at the fruits of my 'playtime' will lead the reader to new directions or stir up further ideas for new variations on this theme. Perhaps it will lead to a new way of approaching design. Tell me, can you feel what is missing? A couple's vow of commitment.

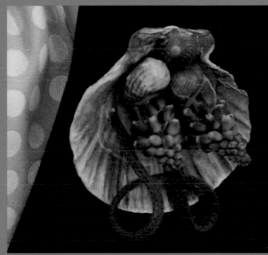

Adenanthos cygnorum
Eremophila nivea
Eucalyptus
Eustoma grandiflorum
Leucojum aestivum
Lupinus texensis 'Texas Bluebonnet'
Mentha piperita 'Black Peppermint'
Muscari armeniacum
Origanum dictamnus
Polypodium punctatum 'Grandiceps'
Salvia horminum
Senecio hybridus
Tillandsia usneoides
Trachymene caerulea
Viola tricolor

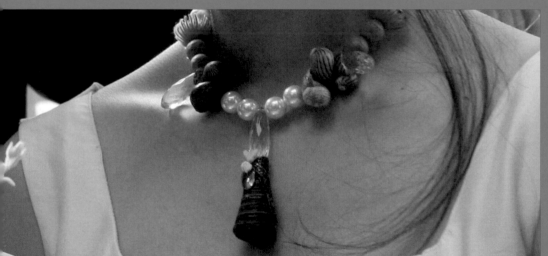

Adenanthos cygnorum
Eremophila nivea
Eucalyptus
Eustoma grandiflorum
Leucojum aestivum
Lupinus texensis 'Texas Bluebonnet'
Mentha piperita 'Black Peppermint'
Muscari armeniacum
Origanum dictamnus
Polypodium punctatum 'Grandiceps'
Salvia horminum
Senecio hybridus
Tillandsia usneoides
Trachymene caerulea
Viola tricolor

Adenanthos cygnorum
Asplenium nidus
Brassica oleracea
Eucalyptus
Eustoma grandiflorum
Ficus pumila
Gaultheria shallon
Gerbera 'Green Spike'
Helleborus foetidus
Lathyrus odoratus
Leucocoryne coquimbensis
Ornithogalum umbellatum
Ranunculus asiaticus
Rosmarinus officinalis
Trifolium arvense

Rosa 'Ranuncula'
Rosa 'Tamango'
Tulipa 'Barbados'
Tulipa 'Holland Happening'
Viburnum opulus 'Compactum'

Astilbe arendsii
Convallaria majalis
Fritillaria verticillata
Hippeastrum 'Apple Blossom'
Lathyrus odoratus
Nigella damascena
Parthenocissus 'Sugarvine'
Ranunculus asiaticus

Cornus alba
Eucalyptus
Lachenalia aloides
Origanum dictamnus
Tulipa
Viburnum opulus 'Compactum'

Centaurea moschata
Eremophila nivea

Allium sphaerocephalum
Hippeastrum 'Chico'
Lachenalia carnosa

Ammi majus
Asparagus densiflorus 'Myers'
Bouvardia
Buxus microphylla 'Japonica'
Lathyrus odoratus
Polyscias fruticosa
Ranunculus asiaticus
Rubus trifidus

Ageratum houstonianum
Astrantia carniolica
Cyperus isocladus
Eryngium
Eucalyptus gunnii
Gerbera
Kalanchoe
Polyscias fruticosa
Ranunculus asiaticus
Rumohra adiantiformis

Bessera elegans | Convallaria majalis |
Eucalyptus 'Tetragona' | Muscari ameniacum |
Rosa 'Little Woods'

Amaranthus caudatus | Brunia stokoei |
Kalanchoe blossfeldiana | Pieris japonica |
Ranunculus asiaticus | Senecio cineraria |
Skimmia japonica | Zantedeschia 'Purple Star'

Helichrysum diosmifolium |
Rosa 'Little Silver' | Senecio cineraria

Edwin R. Molenaar was born in 1966, in Alkmaar, Holland. One day, as a child, he became fascinated by a judo training group practicing near the beach. From that day on, he started longing for Japan, devoted himself to Judo and dreamed of becoming a Ninja. At the same time, he was taught by his grandfather to understand the world of animals and plants. He is like many of the small creatures he once cared for, in that, even today, his sharp curiosity never flags, from morning to night. This inquisitiveness has resulted in the dismantling of many things, trying to find out how they were built (and occasionally how to reassemble them).

In his teens he began handcrafting many things — from a motorcycle to a terrarium for snakes and a refrigerated room for a flower shop. He started his career at that same flower shop, but true opportunity came in his school days, when he started helping out his former teacher with occasional floral projects. This was the real start of his love for floral design: after seeing how much his creations pleased the customer, he decided to become a floral designer.

Edwin Molenaar believes that designers should care about the smallest details of their lifestyle. He has been living in Japan for more than 20 years, always creating new things and managing to evolve each day.

Expressing Vows, it would not have been possible without...

All the Brides and Grooms: I wish to thank you and your families for allowing me inside your private ceremonies and for consenting to share these design ideas with others. I am deeply grateful for your understanding and enthusiasm in this project. **Fred Chevalking:** Were it not for you, I would now be living in the Amazon jungle. Thank you for introducing me to the beauty of flowers, for teaching me how to arrange them and how to serve both flowers and customers. **Kaori Molenaar:** You have always believed in me and you have supported me, regardless, in each new, wild journey. I honour your tremendous patience. **My team:** You have made this book possible by taking over my daily work so I could concentrate on this project. **Stichting Kunstboek:** Incredible, right from the beginning, and, if this is possible, even more patient than my wife. **Hotel Bleston Court/Risonare:** Being able to work in Hotel Bleston Court and Risonare is like working in a dream. Thank you all for your support. **Jeff Cannaday:** I would have been lost in a jungle of words — amazing how you've put my thoughts on paper. **Gerco Westerbeek (Jasfa bv):** Thank you for your help in Holland. **Tomoyuki Sasaki:** Your talent has brought a new dimension to my work. **Marc Dorleijn:** Amazing how you fitted in with the team in Holland right away.

Concept
Edwin R. Molenaar

Photography
Tomoyuki Sasaki
Marc Dorleijn
Randy R.A. Gibbs
Edwin R. Molenaar

Final editing
Heidi Goeminne
Heide-Mieke Scherpereel

Lay-out & print
Group Van Damme, Oostkamp (B)

Published by
Stichting Kunstboek bvba
Legeweg 165
B-8020 Oostkamp (B)
Tel. +32 50 46 19 10
Fax +32 50 46 19 18
info@stichtingkunstboek.com
www.stichtingkunstboek.com

ISBN 978-90-5856-257-9
D/2008/6407/2
NUR 421

© Stichting Kunstboek 2008

Expressing Vows, it would not have been possible without...

All the Brides and Grooms: I wish to thank you and your families for allowing me inside your private ceremonies and for consenting to share these design ideas with others. I am deeply grateful for your understanding and enthusiasm in this project. **Fred Chevalking:** Were it not for you, I would now be living in the Amazon jungle. Thank you for introducing me to the beauty of flowers, for teaching me how to arrange them and how to serve both flowers and customers. **Kaori Molenaar:** You have always believed in me and you have supported me, regardless, in each new, wild journey. I honour your tremendous patience. **My team:** You have made this book possible by taking over my daily work so I could concentrate on this project. **Stichting Kunstboek:** Incredible, right from the beginning, and, if this is possible, even more patient than my wife. **Hotel Bleston Court/Risonare:** Being able to work in Hotel Bleston Court and Risonare is like working in a dream. Thank you all for your support. **Jeff Cannaday:** I would have been lost in a jungle of words — amazing how you've put my thoughts on paper. **Gerco Westerbeek (Jasfa bv):** Thank you for your help in Holland. **Tomoyuki Sasaki:** Your talent has brought a new dimension to my work. **Marc Dorleijn:** Amazing how you fitted in with the team in Holland right away.

Concept
Edwin R. Molenaar

Photography
Tomoyuki Sasaki
Marc Dorleijn
Randy R.A. Gibbs
Edwin R. Molenaar

Final editing
Heidi Goeminne
Heide-Mieke Scherpereel

Lay-out & print
Group Van Damme, Oostkamp (B)

Published by
Stichting Kunstboek bvba
Legeweg 165
B-8020 Oostkamp (B)
Tel. +32 50 46 19 10
Fax +32 50 46 19 18
info@stichtingkunstboek.com
www.stichtingkunstboek.com

ISBN 978-90-5856-257-9
D/2008/6407/2
NUR 421

Edwin R. Molenaar was born in 1966, in Alkmaar, Holland. One day, as a child, he became fascinated by a judo training group practicing near the beach. From that day on, he started longing for Japan, devoted himself to Judo and dreamed of becoming a Ninja. At the same time, he was taught by his grandfather to understand the world of animals and plants. He is like many of the small creatures he once cared for, in that, even today, his sharp curiosity never flags, from morning to night. This inquisitiveness has resulted in the dismantling of many things, trying to find out how they were built (and occasionally how to reassemble them).

In his teens he began handcrafting many things — from a motorcycle to a terrarium for snakes and a refrigerated room for a flower shop. He started his career at that same flower shop, but true opportunity came in his school days, when he started helping out his former teacher with occasional floral projects. This was the real start of his love for floral design: after seeing how much his creations pleased the customer, he decided to become a floral designer.

Edwin Molenaar believes that designers should care about the smallest details of their lifestyle. He has been living in Japan for more than 20 years, always creating new things and managing to evolve each day.